The A
Snou

E.G. ROWLAND

Illustrations by Jonah Jones,
Foreword by John Disley

*Indication of a route in this book
does not imply a right of way.*

First published by Cidron Press, 1956
Second Edition   1960
Third Edition   1967
Fourth Edition   1973 by Vector Publications
Fifth Edition — 1975 by Cicerone Press

Other Guides by Cicerone Press
HILL WALKING IN SNOWDONIA
LLANBERIS AREA GUIDE
WINTER CLIMBS, NORTH WALES
MODERN TECHNIQUES OF SNOW AND ICE
THE ISLAND OF RHUM

Cover: Snowdon from Llyn Padarn   Photo: E.Emrys Jones

SBN 902 363 13 1

Published by Cicerone Press,
16 Briarfield Road, Worsley, Manchester

Snowdon from the West   Photo R. B. Evans

INDEX

FOREWORD

So you're going to climb Snowdon? Well, you won't be the first or the last.

Snowdon attracts the visitor to North Wales as no other mountain does. Whether it's the tourist in his blazer or her flowered skirt, or the cyclist in his corduroy shorts, or the hill-walker in her nailed boots, or the climber with his nylon rope and ice-axe, all of them will gravitate to Yr Wyddfa.

How fortunate that Snowdon, the highest mountain in England and Wales is also the most impressive, set as it is amongst lakes, ridges and cliffs.

How fortunate, too, that we had Mr. Rowland to help us gain full enjoyment from the mountain. This booklet is most comprehensive and straightforward. Even to read the graphic descriptions of the climbs makes me re-live the views and charms of Snowdon.

The mountain is there. The routes to the summit are there. Here is the guide to get you there.

John Disley.

INTRODUCING SNOWDON

Snowdon from near Capel Curig

SNOWDON (3561) is the highest peak south of the Border. It certainly looks a mountain from all points of the compass. Perhaps the best view is the one that greets the eye of visitors coming up A5, Telford's fine old road from Shrewsbury to Holyhead. Where it turns at Capel Curig, travellers passing on to the west, granted a fine day, see a serrated line of peaks along the skyline. In the centre, well above the others, is Snowdon, the king of them all.

That is from the east. From the south is a single cone, rising above its small neighbour Aran (2451). Where the Caernarvon—Portmadoc road passes Penygroes, it is seen from the west in the centre of a wide valley, with satellites on either side. From Llanberis on the north-west, its peak rises behind a tumbled mass of mountains, almost hidden by its nearest rival, Crib y Ddysgl (3493).

As the region is explored, it will be found that five rocky ridges radiate from the summit. Between them are five dark cwms, mainly with sunless depths, that give a forbidding aspect to the approaches. For Snowdon has no sylvan graces. Once the valleys are left behind, it is a treeless waste. There is little heather on its slopes and the grey grass on its less stony sides gives scant nourishment to the hardy mountain sheep that roam on its barren sides. But there is a beauty in this wildness and the many lakes that lie in its cwms and the small streams that run down into them help to relieve the stern landscape.

From the summit cairn there is a wide prospect, the commanding height ensures this. Beyond the nearer grim ridges and hollows, the eye is carried far over land and sea. Thomas Pennant, whose *"Tours in Wales"* was published in 1784, was a visitor here. As with most early climbers, he deemed a guide needful. They started on horseback up the valley that lies under the present railway track. Near the lake at the far end they dismounted and clambered to the upper part of the Snowdon Ranger (II). Reaching the top at an early hour, he thus describes the scene:

"Yr Wyddfa (the Welsh name of Snowdon), rises almost to a point or at best there is but room for a circular wall of stones, within which travellers usually take their repast. The prospect was disclosed like the gradual drawing up of a curtain at a theatre. We saw more and more, till the heat became so powerful as to attract the mists from the various lakes, which in a slight degree obscured the prospect. . . .

I saw the county of Chester, the high hills of Yorkshire, part of the north of England, Scotland and Ireland, a plain view of the Isle of Man, and that of Anglesey lay extended like a map beneath me".

He certainly had good eyesight! He made more than one ascent and regarding another occasion he wrote:

"On this day the sky was obscured very soon after I got up. A vast mist enveloped the whole circuit of the mountain. The prospect down was horrible. It gave the idea of numbers of abysses, concealed by a thick smoke, furiously circulating about us. Very often a gust of wind formed an opening in the clouds, which gave a fine and distinct vista of lake and valley . . . exhibiting a most strange and perplexing sight of waters, fields, rocks or chasms in fifty different places. Then they closed at once and left us involved in darkness".

Today the weather is as changeable as it was in the eighteenth century, but whether you meet clear skies, clouds or mist, you will be well rewarded for your efforts to get a little nearer heaven.

A word about the name of the mountain. Snowdon is a simple English title, now so well embedded in the language that it has usurped the old Welsh names. These were: Eryri, the abode of eagles, birds no longer haunting its crags; and Yr Wyddfa, the great mound or tomb, since the legendary Rhita Fawr is reputed to have been buried on this lofty spot.

Now our pages must turn to the task in hand. After describing a tour round the mountain, they proceed to give details of the five well marked regular paths up the mountain, the Mountain Railway and the famous Horseshoe Walk. They then deal with a few of the lesser used variations from the beaten track, that can be used without gymnastics, and then conclude by giving a few hints to budding hill walkers, which ought to be read and absorbed before setting foot on the mountains themselves.

6

Snowdon from Capel Curig   Photo Eric L. King

A TOUR ROUND SNOWDON

ALL good Alpinists examine a peak before they tackle it. This section is devoted to a tour round Snowdon to give some idea of its surroundings. It is an easy trip by car or cycle and can even be done by a series of buses in the summer season. On foot it is not to be recommended, since the distance is 35 miles, all on main roads.

Starting from Caernarvon, with its grand castle and busy shops, take the Beddgelert road and in a few miles go through the village of Waenfawr. Soon the road passes between high hills. After Bettws Garmon, there is a small wood with charming waterfalls, well tended by a resident who welcomes visitors. Then comes Llyn Cwellyn (464), the largest lake in the Snowdon area. Halfway along its shores is the Snowdon Ranger Youth Hostel. Here is the starting place of a popular route up the mountains (II).

As you rise to the grey village of Rhyd Ddu, you have to the left a very fine view of Snowdon and may see the train puffing its way slowly to the summit or sliding down over its cogs to Llanberis.

Rhyd Ddu has an inn, a cafe and modest accommodation for visitors. Just beyond it on the left was the deserted station of the old Welsh Highland Railway (626). Here is a new parking place for those using the Rhyd Ddu Path (III). A mile on there is a bridge and Pitts Head, a rock with a striking outline of the famous statesman's profile. Close by is the farm track that marks the start of the alternative route from Beddgelert (III). Snowdon is now hidden and there follows a three-mile coast down to Beddgelert. One mile short of the village is the best camping site in the district. It is run by the Forestry Commission, with a room for wet weather, wash houses and a small natural bathing pool. There are varied and secluded spots for tents and caravans and the place is most central for exploring some interesting country. The new forests have sylvan paths and many peaks other than Snowdon are within easy reach.

Beddgelert is a most popular mountain village, with accommodation of every kind. Its only drawback is its lowly situation (125). Our route does not cross the bridge, but goes on through the upper reaches of the beautiful Vale of Nantgwynant. Soon comes Dinas Emrys, a high mound with legends of King Arthur and Merlin. Then we come to Llyn Dinas, a lake in a fine setting. Passing a Holiday Fellowship Home, the

9

road runs down to a bridge over the Glaslyn River. Just short of this is a gate, that marks the start of the Watkin Path (IV).

Here we have the first view of the summit since leaving Pitts Head and a very fine view it is. Looking up a narrow valley, one sees on the skyline a steady rise from the west leading up to the summit and then a sharp drop shows the steepest side of the mountain.

The double peak of Lliwedd (2947) now cuts off the view as Llyn Gwynant is reached. Halt on its lovely shores to gaze up green Cwmdyli, with the plateau of the Glyders behind it. On the right, overlooking the foot of the lake is Bryn Gwynant Youth Hostel. The road rises for three miles to Penygwryd Hotel (886). A mile short of the hotel, look for the finest view of the Snowdon Massif to be had from any main road.

Penygwryd has been the haunt of climbers since the days when it was a modest inn. Charles Kingsley. Tom Hughes and other early mountain lovers were the pioneers of generations of ramblers. Since it was modernised, early this century, its population has increased. The Everest team used it as a base for some of their training and some of them often return to it. It is a main centre for rescue work and is fully equipped for this. The present owner, Mr. Briggs has led many a party to bring in the fallen. Hard by is an artificial lake, Llyn Lockwood, named after a well-known resident, who made it to afford visitors some angling on wet days.

Rising another mile, the top of Llanberis Pass is reached (1169), the highest point of the round. Here stands Penypass Youth Hostel, once a famous hotel, properly called Gorphwysfa (rest and be thankful). It is another busy starting place for ramblers and climbers. Its car park is crowded on fine days and its cafe refreshes many a weary traveller. It, too, has its memories. The list of famous names in mountain history that have sheltered here is a very long one, including H. O. Jones, Mallory, Amery, Arnold Lunn and Winthrop Young. This historic spot is the taking off place for the steepest and shortest path to the top of our mountain, the Pig Track (V).

Now comes a seven mile descent through the grim Pass of Llanberis with high cliffs rising on either side. Just beyond the Cromlech Bridge on the way down, the Climbers' Club have a climbing hut, Ynys Ettws. On the bridge leading to it is a memorial to members that fell in the last war. Near this, by the farm, Blaen-y-Nant, a faint path leads up to the recess of Cwm Glas (VII). Soon the higher hills are left behind and the road levels out through the hamlet of Nant Peris. Next comes Llyn Peris, the higher of the two Llanberis Lakes.

After Dolbadarn Castle, Llanberis is entered by the spacious Victoria Hotel, nearly opposite the lower terminus of the Snowdon Mountain Railway. Near by is the start of the Llanberis Path (I). A short detour should be made from this end of the town to see the fine waterfall where the waters of Afon Arddu drop from the heights to join the lakes. On the other side of the lakes rise, tier over tier, the vast ledges of waste from the big slate quarries that have been worked for centuries. The main part of the little town lies along the lower lake, Llyn Padarn. In it all visitors can find accommodation and its Youth Hostel is well patronised. As you pass along the west side of Llyn Padarn, pause at one of the "lay-bys" to have a last look up the Pass. The lake, the small conifers, the bare rocks on the lower slopes and the high peaks beyond, recall the valleys of Switzerland, more especially in winter when snow mantles the heights. Little remains to be done. Passing over undulating ground, through a village or two Caernarvon is reached in seven miles from Llanberis.

1. THE LLANBERIS PATH

The Llanberis Path

This is the easiest, longest and most popular of the five well-beaten paths up the mountain. It is about five miles from base to summit and is well graded   It more or less follows the railway track from Llanberis.

In Llanberis go to the lower terminus of the railway, with its big car park, crowded in the high season. Pass and

11

turn right, down a short road to a small square. At the far end of this is a gate. Go on through it and start the actual climb up a roughish by-road, with the railway on the right and a few scattered cottages. Soon the path turns left and goes gently on and on with a steady rise, rather damp in places. It dips under the railway and, after an almost level stretch, reaches Halfway House. Here the same family has provided generations of climbers with welcome refreshment, before they tackle the harder part of the journey. Resuming the task, there is, well below on the right, one of the fine cwms that lie between the ridges of the mountain. This is Cwm Brwynog, with a lake, Llyn Du'r Arddu, in its depth. It has a string of small tarns at one end, making it look like a gigantic tadpole. Above it rises a sheer wall of cliff providing the most difficult rock climbs in Wales.

As you circle above the cwm, the way again goes under the railway at Clogwyn Station. Here a halt must be called to note the awesome view down into Llanberis Pass, with the steepest side of the Glyders rising on the far side. This is a real reward for the labours so far. The path swings round south under the dome of Crib y Ddysgl (3493) and the finish is close to the railway. On the left is Cwm Dyli, where the two llynau, Glaslyn and Llydaw, shine in the depths below. Then the railway terminus is reached and behind it is the huge summit cairn, said to have been piled up by the ordnance men when surveying the district. Many years ago two large huts stood on it, one with bunks. Then the traveller could come up overnight and have supper, bed, breakfast and a sunrise for the sum of ten shillings. Today the more spacious buildings of the hotel are just below, so that the top of the peak is no longer disfigured.

II. THE SNOWDON RANGER PATH

This route, like the Llanberis Path (I), gives an easy and pleasant ascent. It is shorter and, in the early stages rather damper, but there are no saddles or sheer drops to trouble sufferers from vertigo, and takes its name from the starting point, the Snowdon Ranger (464), now a very popular Youth Hostel. A century ago, George Barrow, that famous wanderer, passed this way and a young man said to him: "A ranger means a guide, sir, my father-in-law is generally termed the Snowdon Ranger because he is a tip-top guide and has named the house after himself".

The path starts just behind the Hostel, crosses the track of the long disused South Snowdon Railway and from a nearby farm rises by zig-zags upwards. These should be followed till the cultivated land is left at a gate. The path now goes more directly through some boggy land and under a power line that leads over a low col to Llanberis. The path is still well marked and rises, with Llyn Ffynnon y Gwas below on the right and gloomy Cwm Clogwyn behind the lake. Then to the left Cwm Brwynog comes into view with the Llanberis Path (I) on its far side. The ridge narrows somewhat and the top of the cliffs of Clogwyn Du'r Arddu is reached.

Snowdon from the west

Here a short detour should be made to the left to look down the sheer side of this grand rock face. From this point the way widens out into a sort of plateau with a gentler gradient. Cross over this for half-a-mile and the Llanberis Path (I) is reached, alongside the railway track, about ten minutes from the top.

This route is some two miles shorter than the Llanberis Path (I) and is certainly the way that is least dangerous in wintry conditions, when hard snow covers the hillsides and ice makes the rocks tricky. Then even the stony plateau can be very slippery. But novices may be comforted to learn that a sheep farmer and his son on horseback reached the railway track just below the summit in the dry summer of 1955.

III. THE BEDDGELERT—RHYD DDU PATH

The double title is due to the fact that there are two starting points to this very popular ascent. Both are on the Beddgelert-Caernarvon road. Above the third milestone from the village, the first commences through a farm road on the right that leads to Ffridduchaf, marked by a group of conifers. Leave the farmhouse and follow a path up behind it, near a wall. In just over half-a-mile, a rough track is met leading to a disused slate quarry. Here the other route is joined.

This starts from the car park on the site of the deserted station of the old Welsh Highland Railway. The car-park is just on the Beddgelert side of Rhyd-Ddu (626). From it a rough by-road rises and, passing a ruined cottage or two and a deep quarry pit, meets the Ffridduchaf path in a mile.

At this junction leave the by-road and turn sharp left to follow a faint path through rocks and boggy ground near a small stream. Going through one gap in a wall, make for another gap higher up. Where a rocky mound is passed there is a roofless ruin of a small house that was, long ago, a Half-way House. An old lady and her son brought up refreshments on ponies for the benefit of earlier ramblers. Soon a third wall is met and the marked path goes through it and curves out round the contour line. A little time can be saved by turning right up the side of the wall. In either case the edge of grim Cwm Clogwyn (II) compels a turn right. Looking down into its depths, one feels that at last a real start has been made on the mountain.

Still on the edge a steeper rise is followed, where countless feet have marked the most tiring section of the way. Then there is a more level stretch along the face of Llechog, with a steep drop on one side and a sharp rise on the other. At its end is Bwlch Main (3000), the famous Saddle, with sheer falls on either side. Few travellers are troubled by this as a car could be driven across the used path. Beyond this, the path corkscrews in and out of rocks with odd patches of grass, where snowdrifts linger in the spring. Finally a cairn is passed, where the Watkin Path (IV) joins up and in 200 yards the cement building of the summit hotel is reached.

IV. THE WATKIN PATH

The three paths already described mainly rise along ridges and so give wide views almost all the way up. The Watkin Path, however, goes through one of the five great cwms that lie between the spurs, before rising to a col and ends in a rough scramble up the final side of the cwm. It is fairly well sheltered, but has the disadvantage of starting at a low altitude (200).

The route is much used by visitors to the Beddgelert area. It commences some three miles from that village on the Capel Curig road. Here is a gate on the left just before a bridge over the Glaslyn. There is a large car park just on the other side of the bridge. At Hafod y Llan farm, part-way up the track there is a good camping site. The track rises beside a white building, the Chalet on the left, and goes on into Cwm-y-Llan, which is called Cwm Tregalan in its upper reaches. Still on the old quarry track, some very fine waterfalls are passed on the right. At their head is a bridge and Plas Cwmllan is reached. This is a ruined house, finally battered by Commandos who used it as a strong point when training for D-day. The path levels out and the Gladstone Rock stands near a mound on the left. It bears inscription in two languages, since it marks the spot where the veteran statesman, at the age of 84, addressed the assembled Welsh nation in 1892. Both he and his vast audience had a stiff pull up to this lofty spot. Leaving the rocky side of Craig Ddu to the right, a disused quarry is soon reached. Be sure to turn sharp right at the rear end of some roofless huts, which were the "barracks" of quarrymen working here long ago. At weekends they skipped over the hills to their homes and favourite chapels.

Snowdon and the Watkin Path

15

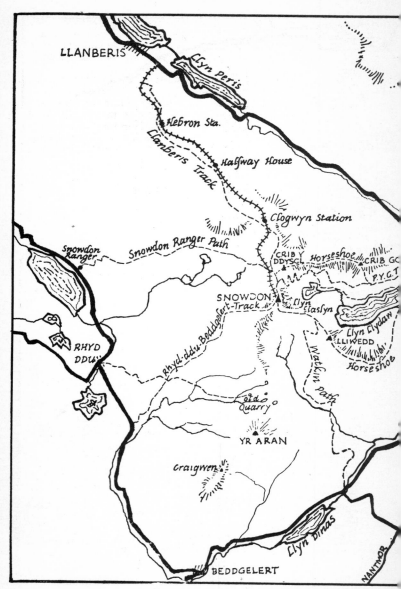

Based upon the Ordnance Survey Map with the sanction of

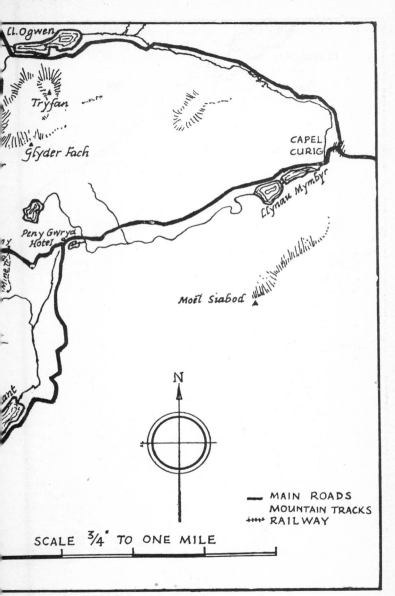

Cl. Ogwen

Tryfan

Glyder Fach

CAPEL CURIG

Llynau Mymbyr

Pen y Gwryd Hotel

Moel Siabod

N

—— MAIN ROADS
MOUNTAIN TRACKS
+++ RAILWAY

SCALE 3/4" TO ONE MILE

A clear but very shaly path now rises, with a kink or two, to the col known as Bwlch y Saethau (Pass of the arrows). This is one of the spots where the legendary King Arthur met his end, being killed by a flight of arrows from a defeated foe descending into Cwm Dyli. When the col is reached, go over to its far edge for a glorious climax to the climb. Cwm Dyli with its three lakes is just below and beyond is a far vista to the east, with the outline of Moel Siabod dominating the centre. Back to the path, there is a level half-mile and then another fine prospect. This is the steepest side of Snowdon. One stands half-way up a sheer drop of 1500 feet, a cliff face that can only be tackled by expert rock climbers.

The finish is up a rough slope of shaly scree. Weathering has almost wiped out the original path and the angle is rather steep. Bear left and it is soon mastered and a cairn on the crest is reached that marks the junction with the Rhyd-Ddu Path (III). In two hundred yards the summit is attained. This route was laid out by Sir Edward Watkin, of the Chalet, to celebrate the visit of Gladstone mentioned earlier. At the same time local quarrymen raised a ten-foot cairn on the top of Lliwedd (VII), the peak just opposite. That too, like the last stages of this path, has almost disappeared.

V. THE PIG TRACK

The path leaves the main road at the top of Llanberis Pass (1169). This lofty start means less actual climbing than from the others. Moreover the route has a varied interest from the first step. Opposite the hostel the way goes right through a gap in the stone wall and under high power poles. At once there is a scramble over well-worn rocks on the north side of the foot hills, with a wide view of Llanberis Pass and the bold cliffs of the Glyders on the other side. Some superfluous cairns mark the path as it goes on over rocky patches and boggy ground, till it bears left to reach Bwlch Moch. Halt here for another wide vista. Below is Llyn Llydaw, with its causeway and behind the lake rise the steep cliffs of Lliwedd, the haunt of the rock climber. To the right is the Snowdon Massif, encircling the gloomiest cwm in Wales.

Behind Bwlch Moch rises the steep way up Crib Goch (VII), but our path drops a little to a fairly level clear track under the mountain's south side. In steady work for over a mile, the old Britannia Copper Mine is reached. It is right above Llyn Glaslyn, the source of the river that runs down into the sea at Portmadoc. The old workings may be explored with some care at an open shaft. Ardent souls have made a steep path over loose scree from the end of the mine to the crest of the col, but wise folk will return to the entrance of the mine and keep well to the right away from the summit. With luck a cairn will be found at the foot of the famous zig-zags. These furnish a much easier way to the second cairn that marks the top of the col. With a sigh of relief, you will join the Llanberis Path (I) at this point and, turning left, proceed along the track or by the nearby footpath to reach the top in about ten minutes.

SOME TRAVERSES

Many ramblers do not like retracing their steps and the following traverses are suggested for those not tied to a parked car or cycle.

(1). Up the Llanberis Path (I) and down the Watkin Path (IV). A long tramp but straightforward throughout, with very little scrambling.

(2). Up the Pig Track (V) and down the Beddgelert-Rhyd Ddu Path (III). The shortest and perhaps the best, since the sunset is faced on the downward way.

(3). Up the Snowdon Ranger Path (II) and down the Watkin Path (IV). This means some road work to Beddgelert at the finish during the off season.

(4). The Rhyd-Ddu Path (III) and the Snowdon Ranger Path (II) can be combined by those with their own transport, since the starting points are not much more than a mile apart.

VI. THE SNOWDON MOUNTAIN RAILWAY

The Snowdon Mountain Railway is obviously the easiest way up the mountain, as the whole ascent is made sitting down. It serves a very useful purpose since it allows invalids, cripples, octogenarians, and the bone lazy to enjoy the pleasures of wide views with no muscular effort. Moreover the weary and those caught in heavy weather on this side of the mountain can take its shelter, since there are four intermediate stations.

Trains run from Easter if the weather is suitable and carry on well into the autumn. There is a timetable, but in the high season, when queues are formed by waiting passengers, the service is almost continuous in daylight. The journey takes about an hour each way. Trains are also run at any time for repair work or in emergencies. They are only halted by very heavy gales, deep snowdrifts or ice choking the cogs on the central rail. At the top is a licensed hotel, just below the summit cairn, with a large hall to shelter passengers. Light refreshments are provided and souvenirs, topical books and picture postcards are on sale. The last can be stamped with a special postmark — "Summit of Snowdon".

The railway is the only one in Britain worked by the rack rail system, based on Swiss design. Between the ordinary rails (gauge 2ft. 7½ins.), is a set of double cogs that engages exactly with pinions on the train, so that it is pulled up literally tooth by tooth. The engine is always at the lower end of the train and the braking is naturally powerful and foolproof. The engines are steam driven with curious sloping boilers. The line is a little under five miles long and rises throughout with no level stretches.

In 1896 the railway was first opened for traffic, but a slight accident showed the need for adjustments. From 1897 trains have gone up and down without incident or accident. Some years ago the brakes were severely tested when a 'plane crashed just before a descending train. They did not fail. Passengers can ride up the steep inclines with no qualms and devote their whole attention to the glorious scenery.

VII. THE HORSESHOE WALK

Before giving a few variations from the usual paths, an outline of the finest ridge walk in Wales must be given. In fact it is rather more than a walk and should not be attempted before a little practice on the hills. If new to the sport, a companion should be taken, an old hand if possible. In any case choose a clear day in summer. In mist it loses its charm and in winter it is often quite an Alpine expedition. Under the best circumstances some scrambling is needed.

An anti-clockwise direction gives most of the hard work in the early stages, a great advantage, so that is the way now described. The start is from Penypass (V), and the Pig Track is used for the first mile. When Bwlch Moch is reached, leave the Track and turn right up a fairly well marked path through some rocks and then come to a much steeper rise up the east face of Crib Goch (3023). On the way a rather exposed point is reached, near some white quartz sticking out of the rock face, but the holds are well marked and the obstacle should be easily surmounted. Except for a loose surface there are no more difficulties till the narrow eastern peak of the mountain is reached. One of the finest views in Snowdonia opens out. It is too well-known from books of photos and picture post-cards to need description. Now comes the tit-bit of the trip. A sharp knife edge, some 400 yards long, has to be crossed. On the left it sheers down into Cwm Dyli and on the right there is still steeper drop into Cwm Glas. Luckily there are plenty of safe footholds in the less steep side, low enough to allow the use of the crest by gripping hands. Those with weak nerves have been known to cross sitting astride the crest, but very few use this uncomfortable method. At the far end are the famous Pinnacles. One or two can be surmounted without much trouble, but the third or Crazy Pinnacle is best left to experts, since it is easily avoided. Indeed, faint hearts can miss them all by a drop down left, just before the first is reached. Do not go very far down, but follow the boot scratches on the rocks.

Now there is a drop to a fine grassy col, Bwlch Goch, a suitable lunch site. Up again through rocks and small grass patches towards the top of Crib y Ddysgl (3493), second only to Snowdon in height. This peak is sometimes called Carnedd Ugain (Hill of the Twenty), but it is not clear who made up the score. In the rocks keep as far right as the precipice allows, otherwise one can drift down too much and land on the zig-zags of the Pig Track (V), to have a steep pull up to regain the crest. Here as elsewhere, ramblers have worked out varying ways through or round a rocky rise and so one can be a little confused with a choice of routes.

Near the summit the ground opens out and leads to a Ordnance column that takes the place of a cairn. Yet another wide vista greets the eye, with a fine view of Snowdon itself. This is easily reached by dropping down to the railway track and ending on the Llanberis Path (I). After a rest and maybe some refreshment in the hotel, a start is made on the much simpler half of the journey. The top part of the Watkin Path (IV) is used at first, the cairn 200 yards down on the Rhyd Ddu Path (III) showing the way down left. It is rough going till Bwlch y Saethau is reached, giving a well-marked level section. At the far end, where the Watkin Path drops to the right, keep straight on up the edge of Lliwedd (2947). From a perfectly

21

safe way through easy rocks, there is a close-up of a wide stretch of sheer rock face, where hardy souls play pitch and toss with death and usually win. Many consider it the finest part of the fine round, as it gives one the impression of climbing a gigantic cathedral spire.

At the first cairn, for there are two main peaks on the mountain, the country to the south opens out and shows the wooded vale of Nantgwynant, through which the River Glaslyn meanders to the sea at Portmadoc. All along this last crest there is a well marked path, near the top of the cliffs, and one can look across the cwm and note the skyline of the morning's work. Most people dodge the minor third peak, by circling behind it, but look out for a cairn in a grassy hollow beyond it. This marks the place where the path turns left and descends to Llyn Llydaw. It is damp and a bit broken, but make for a shed by the causeway near the northern end of the lake. Reaching this a rough by-road is found. Turn right along it and in rather over a mile, Penypass Hostel is reached.

This is the usual round, but if you want to complete a long day, do not turn down at the cairn, but carry on along the ridge, for an interesting walk of a mile to Gallt Y Wenallt (2032)), the very last nail of the Horseshoe. Here are very steep grass slopes, north and east, but there is a pleasant and varied way to the south-west that leads down to Nantgwynant.

Snowdon from near Portmadoc

VIII. OFF THE BEATEN TRACK

If the regular paths to the summit seem too hackneyed, the broken terrain round them is well worth exploring. Here are some hints for the more adventurous. None of the routes described require the craft of rock climbers, who sally forth draped with ropes and use plimsolls on steep patches. All that is needed is a clear head, a fair sense of balance and some knowledge of route finding.

Starting from Llanberis the path can be avoided by keeping to the road leading under the railway and going up the valley at a lower level. In a mile the farm buildings of Hafodty Newydd are reached and there the road ends. Go straight through rather marshy ground, leaving the stream to the right and then work through some boulders to the shores of Llyn Du'r Arddu, with its tail of tarns. There is now a close up from below of one of the steepest rock faces in Wales.

A choice now offers. By skirting round the cliffs and going up the steep grassy slope right the Snowdon Ranger Path (II) can be joined about a mile from the top. But it is better to go left up an easier rise to meet the Llanberis Path (I) near Clogwyn Station. To avoid the regular path altogether, the top of Crib y Ddysgl (VII) can be visited on the way to the summit. Perhaps this should be left to the return journey. If this is done stick to the edge of the cliffs on the right when the cement column is left and follow along for quite a while. When the precipice eases into more broken ground and looks fit to be tackled without undue risk, make a way down it right along the north end of Cwm Glas, keeping near to small stream, till you reach the main road near Beudy Mawr, some two miles above Llanberis. If this sharp descent does not appeal, continue along the crest of the cliffs, well above the railway line. The going is quite good, mainly on grass and there are fine views of the Pass, missed by path users. However, it is easy to drop down to it at any point, but those who like a sporting finish can turn down right before the point marked 1322 on the map and scramble through grass and rocks to the road, half-way along Llyn Peris, a mile from Llanberis. From the 1322 point there is an easier descent to the start of the Llanberis Path (I).

Also from Llanberis there is a sporting way up through Cwm Glas. Go up the pass to the entrance to Blaen y Nant farm and across the bridge over the main stream. Work up by the stream marked Cwm Glas Mawr where there are faint traces of a path used by climbers. At the top of the first rise, a semi-circle of cliffs with steep faces seems to offer no through way. Pause a while on the flat section now reached and study them. On the top of one of the faces, which has waterfalls on both sides, is a big boulder that has all the appearance of a squat toad. A way can be made up either side of this face, that to the right being the more interesting. It leads well into the upper side of Cwm Glas, reputed to be the finest of them all and the one where one can be easily lost. In it is a small tarn, just large enough to be coloured on the map. Behind it rises the well-known rock climb on Clogwyn y Person (Parson's Nose, to most), leading up to the upper part of Crib y Ddysgl. Follow the brook from the upper to the lower and larger lake, by a sharp drop. Here is the heart of Cwm and it affords a fine close view of the Crib Goch ridge above (VII). In the season one can watch wanderers crossing it with varying degrees of confidence.

Follow on due south up a steep scree slope with traces of a path, till the skyline is reached at the col Bwlch Goch on the Horseshoe Walk (VII). From this point the way given in (VII) can be followed to the top of Snowdon, or Penypass reached over the summit of Crib Goch. Weary ones can drop down in a very steep slope on grass or scree to the path by the two lakes in upper Cwm Dyli. This should not be attempted when snow or ice is about and, in very dry weather, use the scree that is alongside the grass, which will be too slippery for comfort.

As the lower slopes of Snowdon to the west are relatively open, ramblers from that side need not stick too closely to the paths in the early stages. For those who like a long easy trudge over soft grass there are three miles that can be taken on the descent of the Snowdon Ranger Path (II). It runs along the south skyline of Cwm Brwynog opposite the railway, and is mainly on the 2000 ft. contour line. Turn right when well past Llyn Ffynnon y Gwas and climb up for the wide view from Moel Cynghorion (not named on the map). Then go south-west by the edge of some cliffs and then continue north-west up and down until till the ridge ends at Moel Eilio (2382). The way cannot be missed if you stick to the skyline and there are plenty of places where a descent to the south can be made. But it is worth going on to the final peak to see the lowlands stretching out below. From this point moreover there is an easy descent to Llanberis. Make straight for the colour-washed front of the Victoria Hotel, by a very gentle gradient. On the other side rather more care must be taken to reach the main roads as there are a few sharp drops. This way makes an excellent ascent, as Snowdon lies ahead all the way and there are few steep places. It can be commenced from the village of Waenfawr.

From Rhyd Ddu or Beddgelert (II) there is a pleasing variation. Where the quarry road from Rhyd-Ddu meets the path from Ffridduchaf farm, do not turn left through the small rocks, but continue on up the track till it ends at some old quarry workings, with two small tarns nearby. Here turn left up

Lliwedd and part of the Horseshoe Walk   Photo L. & M. Gayto

a steep slope on grass, where others have left faint traces of a path. Down on the right lies Cwm Tregalon, through which runs the lower part of the Watkin Path (IV). At the top there is a small drop down to the regular path, just short of the Saddle and the route ends as in (III).

In far off days guides used to race from Beddgelert to the top and back for a small prize. Naturally they used the shortest way from the village that runs as follows. Go up the Rhyd Ddu road for a mile and then leave it right for a long pull over grass on the north side of Craig Wen and Aran to the old quarry mentioned above and then mount as described in the last route. There is a footpath in the lower part marked on the map, but the writer has never been able to find it.

A more strenuous way is to go along the Capel Curig road from Beddgelert for a mile-and-a-half and turn left, just short of Llyn Dinas, by the farm, Hafod-y-porth. Leaving the farm on the left and some small cliffs on the right, work up by an old copper mine to the cairn on Aran (2451). This is a splendid viewpoint. The drop is a little too sheer for a direct assault on Snowdon, so a descent to the left must be made to reach the quarry already mentioned in the last two suggestions. By bearing to the left before the last rise, the col between Craig Wen and Aran can be crossed at a lower level, but the extra effort to top Aran is well worthwhile.

The Watkin Path (IV) gives such a fine valley approach that there are only a few variations to suggest. One that is well worth trying starts from the roofless huts well past the Gladstone Rock. Instead of the sharp turn right up the shaly path, go left over the steep grass slopes to the crest above. Here the path up from the upper quarry, so often mentioned in these deviations, will be joined and the finish is over Bwlch Main (III). This is as easy and less stony than the regular route, and can be used either ascending or descending.

Those who like to bag an extra peak can turn right beyond the Gladstone Rock and mount by steep stony pathless slopes to the top of Lliwedd (VII).Thence descend by the edge to Bwlch-y-Saethau and end on the regular Watkin Path (IV). But it is better to take Lliwedd on the way down from Snowdon by a section of the Horseshoe Walk (VII). There is a choice of descents from Lliwedd. In the afternoon it is pleasant to stroll almost due south to the south end of Llyn Gwynant or you can work west to rejoin the Watkin Path near the quarry. In either case it is as well to avoid the cliffs of Craig-ddu.

There is one well-used change from the Pig Track (V),

which is preferable when descending. Use the zig-zags as far as the copper mine, then turn down on a stony steep drop right down to Llyn Glaslyn. On its banks an old quarry road is met that circles the lake and passes some ruined buildings. Where a rushing stream leaves the lake, there is another sharp drop of over 500 feet to Llyn Llydaw. Now all is plain sailing and the weary will enjoy the long level trek by the lakeside, stopping at more ruins, to marvel how some massive iron blocks were brought up so high. Almost at the end of the lake a causeway must be crossed. A word of warning here. The causeway is sometimes under water, so make enquiries before using this route. If caught out, however, there is a way round the northern corner of the lake leading over Penypass. This is said to be the old pony track, but how ponies managed to reach the top is hard to imagine. Yet there are faded photos, taken before the railway was opened, showing a number of them around the summit cairn. Once the causeway is crossed there is only that long level mile on the by-road, just possible for cars, that passes Llyn Teryn on the way to Penypass (VII).

Here is a sporting way up of much merit. Use the rough road from Penypass to Llyn Llydaw as far as the causeway, but do not cross it. Instead keep along the southern side of the lake throughout its whole length. All the way there is a view of the stark cliffs of Lliwedd, possibly with some gymnasts sporting on them. Follow right round the curve at the end of the lake till a grassy hollow is reached near the outfall of the stream coming down from Llyn Glaslyn. Then mount left up a rocky spine that divides the two lakes. Be careful to keep on the crest of the spine, guided by boot scratches on the rocks, left by previous ramblers. If this hint is followed, you will have a jolly scramble with no difficulty. At the top there is a lonely cairn. From it turn west and you will soon find the north end of Bwlch-y-Saethau (IV) and you complete the climb by the last stage of the Watkin Path. The ridge described is known as the Snowdon Gribbin. If you want to descend it, be sure to find that lonely cairn, as it is essential to keep to the "straight and narrow way" as you descend.

Lastly for those coming down over the top of Crib y Ddysgl (VII) who do not want to go over Crib Goch. When you reach Bwlch Goch, just short of the Pinnacles, a descent can be made either to the north into Cwm Glas or to the south down to the Pig Track (V) by routes described earlier in this section.

These suggestions do not cover all possible ascents through the wild and broken cwms and ridges around our peak, but they give some idea of ways that can be used by ordinary ramblers without danger.

HINTS AND TIPS

THIS section can be skipped by those content with a single trip up and down the mountain on a sunny day and by experienced hill walkers. It is intended for beginners who mean to follow up a sport that can be indulged in right on to a ripe old age.

Those straying from the paths should carry a copy of the 1:50,000 Ordnance Survey Map, "Sheet No. 115, as it covers all the ground. The two-and-a-half inch maps are also available, giving greater detail. Sheets SH55 and SH65 cover the centre of the area. This book is based on the former and the spelling of Welsh names follows it closely.

A pocket compass is helpful, especially in misty weather. Walking-sticks get in the way when scrambling has to be done, but an ice-axe should always be carried when there is snow and ice about. Be sure you know how to use it before it is slung over your arm when setting out. Indeed, in wintry conditions, novices should not go up alone but seek the company of an experienced companion.

Your feet will do most of the work and must be looked after. Boots should be stout, waterproof and above all, comfortable. The soles should be of the Vibram or Commando type, with deep cleats. Smooth soles, Tuf boots and the like are dangerous and highly unsuitable. Socks should be thick and if there is room in your boots for two pairs, so much the better. New boots must be broken in slowly, otherwise you are almost sure to end up with painful blisters.

Clothing is very much up to the individual, his budget and the conditions of the day. An absolute essential is a wind and waterproof anorak. The lightest and cheapest are made from nylon cloth, though these tear rather easily. Overtrousers of the same material are useful for heavy rain. A warm pullover should be taken, even on the warmest of days — it is usually much cooler higher up. In cold weather a woollen cap or balaclava and gloves make a vast difference to comfort. Woollen trousers or, preferably, breeches are best. Shorts are totally unsuitable on their own. Even in summer, always take some spare clothing to put on when resting. In winter this is a vital necessity. If in doubt, do not be afraid to ask for advice.

Rucksacks are useful if only to carry spare clothing. Other contents can be left to trial and error, but put in some food, and keep a little in reserve in case you are benighted. Concentrated items such as chocolate or pressed dates are always welcome.

Do not overload your pack and let it be light and frameless, unless you are compelled to carry camping kit.

Duly prepared on these lines you can sally forth. A dash up and down Snowdon can be undertaken forthwith, but if any out-of-the-way excursion is intended, more is needed. Study your route on the map. It will indicate what is practicable, where steep places have to be tackled and where rock faces bar the way. Plans may not be carried out in full, but aimless wanderings are apt to be wearisome.

The weather is an important factor. Many people fix a date in advance for a particular trip and stubbornly stick to it and spend an uncomfortable day in wind and rain, seeing nothing for their pains. Some hardy souls revel in this sort of thing, but the wiser wait for a good day and have a due reward for patience. But even sunny mornings may turn into rainy, misty and windy afternoons. In such a case, it is quite possible to lose one's bearings, especially in open country or the wider cwms. Then a compass is useful, but bearings must be taken from an exactly known spot to be of service, so do not wait till visibility is narrowed to a few yards. The wise wanderer always notes landmarks and keeps his eye on the sun for a general direction. If really stumped, the lay of the land will help and if a retreat is decided on, it is often possible to follow a stream. If it should plunge over a high cliff as a waterfall, a little scouting on either side usually finds a practicable way to lower levels.

Keep to a steady pace throughout, especially avoiding haste in the early stages. Be a tortoise rather than a hare. A party should *always* stick together regulating its pace to that of its slowest member. Rest at fairly frequent intervals to enjoy the scenery, rather than take an exhausted interval after a long pull to the summit. Do not imitate the scorching cyclist with head bent over down-curved handlebars.

In unknown country keep an eye on the terrain ahead. Try to pick out grass slopes that often reach right up to the top. Avoid patches of bracken on the lower slopes. They are toilsome to wade through and they are often waist-high in summer. Bogs are found at all levels and should be circumvented if possible, for the sake of dry feet. They are only dangerous in a very few cases. Sheep beat down narrow tracks in some places and these may be of use if a detour is not possible. Heather is no great obstacle, indeed it offers fairly safe handholds on steep places, since its roots are deep. When bracken and heather cover big boulders, tread very carefully. Scree too is toilsome to ascend and can only be slid down easily when the stones in it are small. Do any scrambling most cautiously. Always test handholds by a strong pull, before any weight is trusted to them. Be sure there is a reasonable way to the top of any steep face before starting it. It is difficult to turn back once committed, as one cannot see a downward way as easily as an upward one. Take the best footholds available and stand well out from the rock to afford better balance.

If any uncertainty arises, do not be ashamed to turn back. There is no pleasure in exposure for hours in bleak uplands. Wind, too, can be an enemy when at gale force. Often the slope allows for progress along the leeside of a ridge, when use of the crest is troublesome or even dangerous. The edge of cliff faces should be avoided at these times. Use care on wet rocks and on steep grass slopes whether wet or slippery in a heat wave.

In the winter glorious walks can be enjoyed, but every care must be taken to avoid accidents. Often the snow lies in deep drifts and forms cornices along the crests, that hide the real edge most deceptively. There may be snow frozen so hard that the foot does not break through and a slip may start a slide that ends disastrously. Stick to known tracks, take a companion and retreat at once should mist descend or a gale blow up.

Accidents are becoming rather too frequent in these hills. The main cause is the growing number of novices wandering in high places. The majority of casualties are minor ones, such as sprained ankles, cuts and bruises. A small package of plasters and bandages in the rucksack helps in such cases. Do not remove the boot in the case of a sprained ankle. Lace it tightly and bandage well above it. The patient should then be able to hobble down. Should serious injury prevent further progress, shelter the victim and cover him with all spare garments available. If at all possible, leave someone with him, while a message is sent down for a rescue party. There are Rescue Posts at Penygwryd Hotel (Llanberis 211), and, further away, at Ogwen Cottage Outdoor Pursuits Centre (Bethesda 214). A phone message to Llanberis police will bring help (Llanberis 222).

Recent observation compel me to draw special attention to the simple rules of the Country Code: Guard against fire; fasten all gates; keep dogs under control; never walk on growing crops (including hay); avoid damaging fences, hedges and walls; and *leave no litter*. To these may be added a point specially applicable to these parts: never indulge in the childish habit of rolling boulders down slopes. Respect the dry stone walls that divide the sheep-walks. They are easily damaged if you clamber over them. A detour to the nearest gate can usually be made. Finally the words in italics need emphasis, particularly of late. Remember the words of G. M. Trevelyan, O.M.: "The litter that one party of tourists selfishly leaves behind, destroys the pleasure of the next visitors".

L'ENVOI

Speaking of the vulgar crowds on Snowdon, a fastidious author writes: "It is perhaps as well that one mountain should be sacrificed to make a British holiday". There is an answer to this narrow view.

Snowdon will not lose its grandeur even if vaster multitudes visit its heights; the lover of solitude has many a nearby peak where he can wander alone the livelong day and it is no bad thing to meet a number of your fellowmen, enjoying themselves on a spacious hillside.

E. G. ROWLAND

Llynau Glaslyn and Llydaw from the summit